C000001370

ing to sleep. The shadows are
ain. From the russet slopes of
e bleating of lambs & the sound
rying on the strand. I am,
night. My spirit yearns to
is worry on my mind & the
to a country where I would
úras go tír na n-óg - journey to the land of youth

TO THE WEST

ike a gentle zephyr whispering
to my ship & loosen the sail
afely. I do not wish for a land
r a land full of friendship &
exists among the intelligentsia
travelling, to the land of youth.

CELTIC BOOK OF DAYS

Celtic

BOOK OF DAYS

ILLUSTRATED BY
Lynne Muir

TEXT SELECTED BY
Louis de Paor

THE O'BRIEN PRESS
DUBLIN

INTRODUCTION

The fragments of poetry and prose reproduced in this book of days provide glimpses of some of the greatest moments in literature in the Celtic tradition, from the time when writing was first introduced to the Celtic world, through to the present time. While I have chosen the material entirely from the Irish-Gaelic tradition for the sake of unity and coherence, the world-view conveyed here is based on a shared system of perception and belief that informs the Celtic imagination, whatever its geographic location. The stories and poems follow the course of Irish-Gaelic literature, from the pre-Christian sagas of the heroic world to the ground-breaking work of con-temporary poets such as Nuala Ní Dhomhnaill and Cathal Ó Searcaigh. I have included excerpts  from the marvelous nature poetry of the monastic tradition, the early bardic, or court, poetry, and the unfettered love songs of the emergent folk tradition.

The continuity of imagination in this literature gives the individual voices of writers centuries removed from each other the force of an accumulated tribal utterance speaking to us across boundaries of time and space. I have given some indication of that coherence of imagination in the notes that introduce the months of the calendar.

Framed by the Irish and Welsh names for the individual months, these introductory notes briefly explore the themes of sovereignty, religion, place-lore, love, transformation and integration, migration, and the otherworld. I have also described some of the rituals and traditions surrounding the great Celtic festivals of Imbolc, Beltene, Lughnasa, and Samhain.

Lynne Muir's artwork is  founded on the same sense of equilibrium between past and present that gives the text its thematic coherence. Her empathy with and understanding of the patterns of continuity and innovation in the Celtic imagination is evident in her choice of imagery and color, her subtle mix of traditional and modern styles of calligraphy, and in her deft manipulation of geometric shapes to further extend the ideas articulated in the text. In this, Lynne's work is entirely in keeping with earlier Celtic practice, showing due deference to tradition while incorporating more contemporary ideas and techniques. As with the work of modern Irish language poets, her reworking of traditional materials indicates the dynamic possibilities of an age-old tradition that is always in the process of being reborn.

Louis de Paor
Uachtar Ard, 1999

According to the myth of SOVEREIGNTY, the man who would be king must first meet & couple with a repulsive hag who represents the local earth goddess in her barren & most formidable aspect. By their union, the rift between the human & the NATURAL WORLDS is healed as the hag is trans— formed into a beautiful young woman symbolizing the fertility of the earth under the rule of a RIGHTFUL king. The sexual liaison between hag & hero reconciles the masculine principle of order with the sometimes contradictory but properly complementary feminine principle of fertility & abundance.

January

1

2

3

4

5

6

7

8

"Mise Éire" ["I am Ireland"] by Pádraig Mac Piarais
twentieth century
trans. Louis de Paor

I AM IRELAND:

I am older than the HAG OF BÉARRA.

GREAT MY GLORY:

It was I who bore brave CÚCHULAINN.

GREAT MY SHAME:

My own children betrayed THEIR MOTHER.

I AM IRELAND:

I am more lonely than the HAG OF BÉARRA.

WHEN CÚCHULAINN
SCORNED HER ASSISTANCE
THE MORRIGAN ANSWERED:

'I'll get under your feet in the
shape of an eel
and trip you in the ford.'

'I'll come in the shape of a
grey she-wolf,
to stampede the beasts
into the ford against you.'

'I'll come before you in the shape
of a hornless red heifer
and lead the cattle herd to
trample you in the waters,
by ford and pool,
and you won't know me.'

January

9

10

11

12

13

14

15

16

from the Irish epic, *Táin Bó Cuailgne* [*The Cattle Raid of Cooley*]
eighth century or earlier
trans. Thomas Kinsella

January

17

18

19

20

21

22

23

24

from "Blodewedd" by Nuala Ní Dhomhnaill
twentieth century
trans. John Montague

At the least touch
of your fingertips
I break into blossom
my whole chemical
composition
TRANSFORMED
I sprawl like a
grassy meadow
fragrant in the sun;
at the brush of your palm,
all my herbs & spices spill open
frond by frond,
lured to unfold,
and exhale in the heat;
wild strawberries rife
and pimpernels
fragrant & scarlet,
blushing
down their stems.

SINCE CONAIRE BECAME KING

NO CLOUD HAS OBSCURED THE SUN FROM THE MIDDLE o ᵱ SPRING TO THE MIDDLE o ᵱ AUTUMN.

NOT A DROP OF DEW FALLS FROM THE GRASS UNTIL NOON; NO GUST OF WIND STIRS A COW'S TAIL UNTIL EVENING.

January

25

26

27

28

29

30

31

from "The Destruction of Da Derga's Hostel"
eighth century or earlier
trans. Jeffrey Gantz
In response to the formidable Ingcél, grandson of Conmac of Bretain, Fer
Rogain indicates how the natural world prospers under the rule of Conaire.

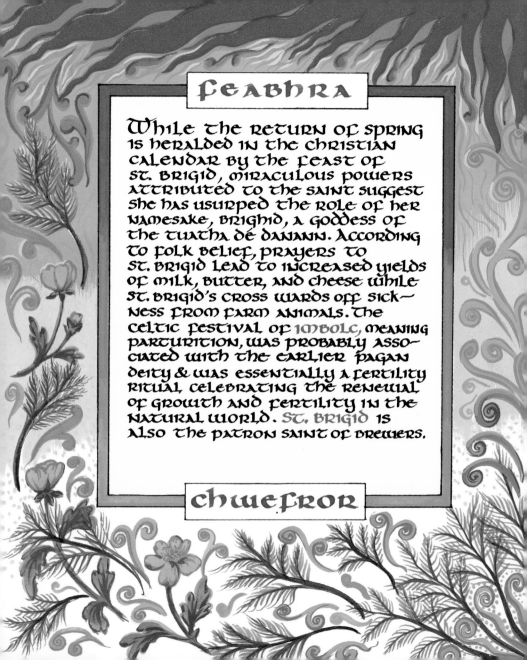

Feabhra

While the return of spring is heralded in the Christian calendar by the feast of St. Brigid, miraculous powers attributed to the saint suggest she has usurped the role of her namesake, Brighid, a goddess of the Tuatha Dé Danann. According to folk belief, prayers to St. Brigid lead to increased yields of milk, butter, and cheese while St. Brigid's cross wards off sickness from farm animals. The Celtic festival of Imbolc, meaning parturition, was probably associated with the earlier pagan deity & was essentially a fertility ritual, celebrating the renewal of growth and fertility in the natural world. St. Brigid is also the patron saint of brewers.

Chwefror

FEBRUARY

1 _____

2 _____

3 _____

4 _____

5 _____

6 _____

7 _____

8 _____

from "Saint Brigid's Prayer," Anonymous
trans. Brendan Kennelly

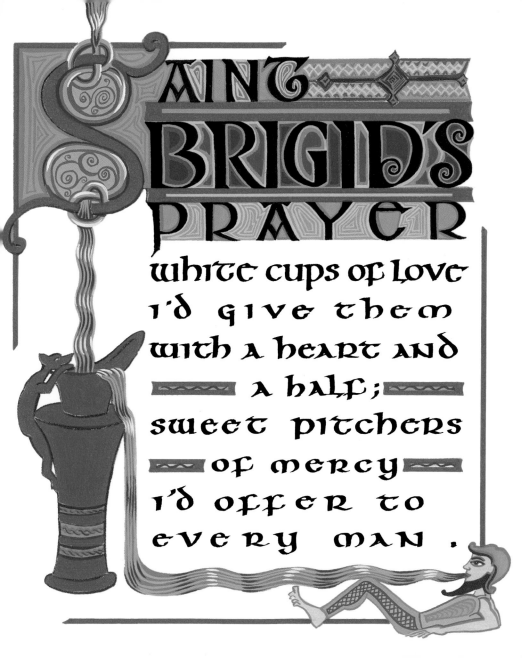

SAINT BRIGID'S PRAYER

white cups of love
i'd give them
with a heart and
a half;
sweet pitchers
of mercy
i'd offer to
every man .

Like silence
you come from the
morning
mist,
musk of bog-myrtle
on your heather-cloak,
your limbs—
bright streams lapping
joyfully around me,
limbs that
welcome me
with skylarks.

February

9

10

11

12

13

14

15

16

from "Cor Úr" ["A Fresh Dimension"] by Cathal Ó Searcaigh
twentieth century
trans. Gabriel Fitzmaurice

FEBRUARY

17

18

19

20

21

22

23

24

"The Blackbird by Belfast Loch," Anonymous
ninth century
trans. Frank O'Connor

WHAT LITTLE THROAT

has framed that note?
what gold beak shot
it far away?

A BLACKBIRD
ON HIS LEAFY
THRONE
TOSSED IT
ALONE ACROSS
THE BAY.

BRIGIT

was born at sunrise, neither within nor without a house, is fed from the milk of a white red-eared cow, hangs her wet cloak on the rays of the sun...

25

26

27

28

29

from *Celtic Mythology* by Proinsias Mac Cana

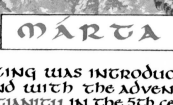

MÁRTA

Writing was introduced to Ireland with the advent of CHRISTIANITY in the 5th century A.D. A century later, material from the older PAGAN world was being recorded by clerical scribes, testament to the remarkable rapprochement between the two traditions. While suffering the white martyrdom of exile on the remote island of Iona, ST. COLUMCILLE returned briefly to defend the poetic order, druidic high priests of the celtic world, against an attempt to banish them from Ireland. This ability to straddle two orders of belief, a BENIGN SCHIZOPHRENIA, is characteristic of Irish folk belief where pagan rituals & practices are reconciled with orthodox christian faith.

MAWRTH

March

1 _____

2 _____

3 _____

4 _____

5 _____

6 _____

7 _____

8 _____

Fragment of Old Irish apocryphal story of St. Patrick

WHILE

BAPTISING AENGUS, KING OF MUNSTER, PATRICK PIERCED THE KING'S FOOT WITH HIS CROSIER. WHEN ASKED WHY HE DID NOT CRY OUT, AENGUS ANSWERED THAT HE THOUGHT THE SPEARING PART OF THE INITIATION RITUAL.

"IN IONA that is my HEART'S DESIRE, IONA, that is my LOVE, the LOWING OF COWS shall yet REPLACE the VOICES OF MONKS: BUT BEFORE the END IS COME IONA shall AGAIN BE AS IT WAS.

March

9

10

11

12

13

14

15

16

St. Columcille's prophecy
sixth century
trans. Fiona McLeod

March

17

18

19

20

21

22

23

24

from "The Praise of Fionn," Anonymous
sixteenth century
trans. Frank O'Connor
Fionn is the principal hero in one of the central story cycles
in the Irish tradition referred to as Fiannaíocht.

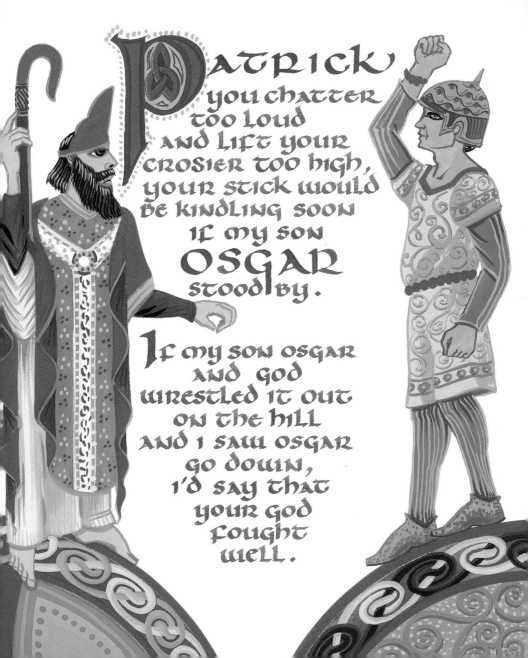

PATRICK
you chatter
too loud
and lift your
crosier too high,
your stick would
be kindling soon
if my son
OSGAR
stood by.

If my son Osgar
and god
wrestled it out
on the hill
and I saw Osgar
go down,
I'd say that
your god
fought
well.

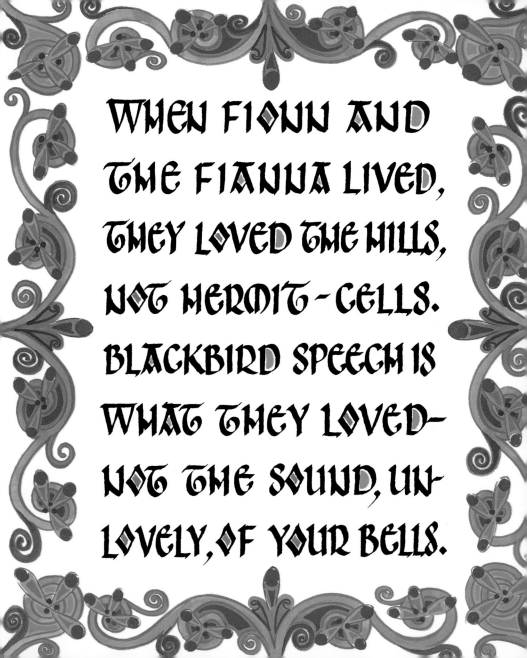

When Fionn and
the Fianna lived,
they loved the hills,
not hermit-cells.
Blackbird speech is
what they loved—
not the sound, un-
lovely, of your bells.

March

25

26

27

28

29

30

31

from "Binn Sin, a Luin Doire an Chairn!"
["Beautiful Blackbird of Doire an Chairn!"], Anonymous
fifteenth century   trans. Thomas Kinsella
On his return from Tír na nÓg, the land of youth, the pre-Christian hero
Oisín laments the passing of the heroic order.

The Dinnseanchas, or place-lore, provides an imaginative record of human & divine interaction with the landscape of Ireland. Every feature of the natural world has its own psychic history— from the Hill of Tara with its kingship cult celebrating the symbolic marriage of king & earth goddess, to the River Boyne, named after a cow-shaped goddess associated with wisdom, and the Two Paps of Danu, which embody the sacred connection between the deity, Danu, and the land of Munster. In the less exalted world of folklore, the local significance of each hill, stream and field is recorded in place-lore, which articulates the community's intimate connection with its ancestral land.

April

1

2

3

4

5

6

7

8

from the Irish epic, *Táin Bó Cuailgne* [*The Cattle Raid of Cooley*]
eighth century or earlier
trans. Thomas Kinsella

QUEEN MEDB

Wherever Medb rested her horsewhip in the district of Cuib, the name Bile Medba, Medb's whip, has remained. ✑

Any ford or height she stopped at is called Medb's ford or Medb's hill. ✑

And one day
in Cathair Léith
a white trout leapt
out of the river
and into the bucket
of a woman
who had led her cows
to water there;

a time when three ships
came sailing into the bay
the eagle was still nesting
on the top of the hill
and the sheep of Cathair
had spancels of silk.

April

9

10

11

12

13

14

15

16

from "I mBaile an tSléibhe" ["In Baile an tSléibhe"] by Nuala Ní Dhomhnaill
twentieth century
trans. Nuala Ní Dhomhnaill
A contemporary *dinnseanchas* poem in which the poet names her own
ancestral places and locates her identity in stories from that area.

17

18

19

20

21

22

23

24

Old Irish story from the Ulster cycle explaining how
the royal seat at Emain Macha got its name

The Royal Fort of Ulster at EMAIN MACHA

Twins of Macha

Emain Macha

takes its name from Macha who gave birth to twins (emain) prematurely, having been forced to race against the royal horses to make good the boast of her husband, the king, that she could outrun them.

THROAT-SONG

of the **BLACKBIRD** of

DOIRE AN CHAIRN

and the stag's call from aill na gcaor
were fionn's music, sleeping at morn,
and the ducks from loch na dtrí gcaol,

THE GROUSE

at **CRUACHAN,**

seat of conn,

otters whistling at druim dá loch,
eagle cry in gleann na bhfuath,
cuckoos' murmur on cnoc na scoth,...

April

25

26

27

28

29

30

from "Binn Sin, a Luin Doire an Chairn!"
["Beautiful Blackbird of Doire an Chairn!"], Anonymous
fifteenth century
trans. Thomas Kinsella

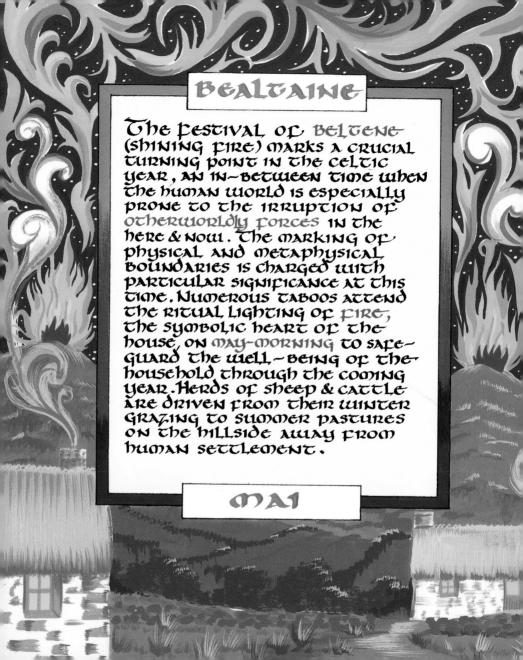

BEALTAINE

The festival of BELTENE (SHINING FIRE) marks a crucial turning point in the Celtic year, an in-between time when the human world is especially prone to the irruption of OTHERWORLDLY FORCES in the here & now. The marking of physical and metaphysical boundaries is charged with particular significance at this time. Numerous taboos attend the ritual lighting of FIRE, the symbolic heart of the house, on MAY-MORNING to safeguard the well-being of the household through the coming year. Herds of sheep & cattle are driven from their winter grazing to summer pastures on the hillside away from human settlement.

MAI

May

1
_____

2
_____

3
_____

4
_____

5
_____

6
_____

7
_____

8
_____

Interpretation of Old Irish tradition

FIRE

AS FIRE SYMBOLIZES THE SUPREMACY OF THE ONE WHO LIGHTS IT, ST. PATRICK SYMBOLICALLY EXTINGUISHED THE POWER OF HIS ADVERSARIES BY LIGHTING THE PASCHAL FIRE BEFORE THE DRUIDIC FIRE AT TARA.

9 _____ ∴

10 _____ ∴

11 _____ ∴

12 _____ ∴

13 _____ ∴

14 _____ ∴

15 _____ ∴

16 _____ ∴

from "Séasúir" ["Seasons"] by Cathal Ó Searcaigh
twentieth century
trans. Cathal Ó Searcaigh

17

18

19

20

21

22

23

24

from "May," Anonymous
ninth century
trans. Frank O'Connor

SUMMER STEMS THE
LANGUID STREAM,
THIRSTY
HORSES
RUSH THE POOL,
BRACKEN
BRISTLES
EVERYWHERE,
WHITE
BOG-COTTON
IS IN BLOOM.

THE
CORNCRAKE
DRONES,
A BUSTLING BARD,
THE COLD CASCADE
THAT LEAPS
THE ROCK
SINGS
OF THE SNUGNESS
OF THE POOL,
THEIR
SEASON
COME,
THE
RUSHES
TALK.

CONFLAGRATION'S FIREBRAND
thaws the film of frost
on the
CALM CLEAR EYE;
THE ICY MANACLES
on his
smooth brown hands—
'tis a red sheet of
FLAME
that melts them.

May

25

26

27

28

29

30

31

from "Fuar liom an adhaighsi dh'Aodh" ["Too cold I deem this night for Hugh"]
by Eochaidh Ó h Eóghusa
seventeenth century
trans. Osborn Bergin

In Celtic Irish tradition there is an emphasis on the physical nature of human love and little sense of spiritual transgression in erotic encounters where the greatest sin is to abandon a loved one. In the older sagas women frequently take the initiative in prosecuting affairs of the heart. In stories such as that of Deirdre & Naoise or Diarmuid & Gráinne, unsanctioned love affairs prompted by the erotic ambitions of a disruptive woman appear to cause chaos & disharmony in the heroic world. Such disorder, however, is more likely the result of a male infringement against the sacred equilibrium between the sexes.

June

1

2

3

4

5

6

7

8

"Aideen," Anonymous
eighth century or earlier
trans. Frank O'Connor

all
are
keen
to
know
who'll
sleep
with
blond
aideen

all
aideen
herself
will
own
is that
she
will not
sleep
alone

Had I

you
without
herds,
without
money or
rich array,
& I'd wed you
on a dewy
morning
at day-
dawn
grey;

bitter
woe it is,
love, that
we are not
far away
in
Cashel
town,
though the
bare deal board
were our
marriage bed
this day.

9

10

11

12

13

14

15

16

from "Caiseal Mumhan" ["Cashel of Munster"], Anonymous
seventeenth century or earlier
trans. Samuel Ferguson

June

17

18

19

20

21

22

23

24

"An Droighneán Donn" ["The Blackthorn Bush"], Anonymous
possibly seventeenth century
trans. James Carney

A HUNDRED MEN
think I am theirs
when I drink wine;

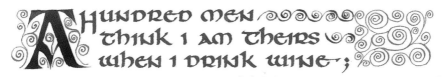

AN DROIGHNEAN DONN

B UT they go away
when I start to think
on your talk & mine.

S LIEVE O'FLYNN IS QUIET,
silent with
snowdrift's hush,

THE BLACKTHORN BUSH

A ND my love is like
sloe-blossom on
the blackthorn bush.

I am stretched on
your grave and
would lie there
forever

if your hands were in mine
I am sure we'd not sever

my apple tree
my brightness
'tis time we were together

for I smell of the earth,
and am worn by the weather.

June

25 _____

26 _____

27 _____

28 _____

29 _____

30 _____

from "Táim Sínte ar do Thuama" ["I Am Stretched on Your Grave"], Anonymous
possibly seventeenth century or earlier
trans. Frank O'Connor

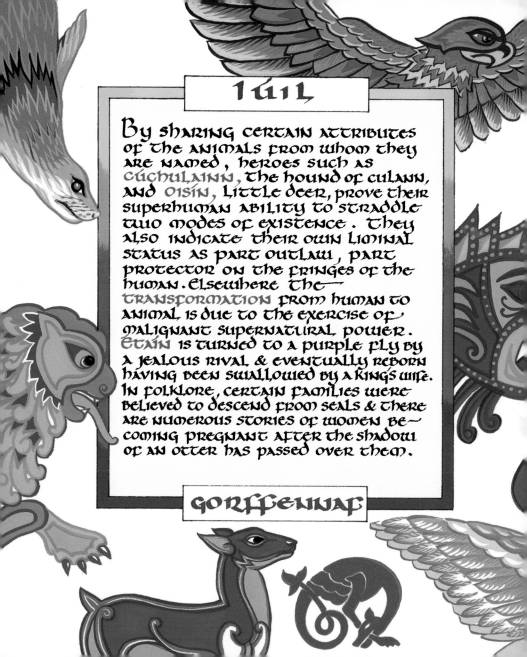

By sharing certain attributes of the animals from whom they are named, heroes such as Cúchulainn, the hound of Culann, and Oisín, little deer, prove their superhuman ability to straddle two modes of existence. They also indicate their own liminal status as part outlaw, part protector on the fringes of the human. Elsewhere the transformation from human to animal, is due to the exercise of malignant supernatural power. Etaín is turned to a purple fly by a jealous rival & eventually reborn having been swallowed by a king's wife. In folklore, certain families were believed to descend from seals & there are numerous stories of women be-coming pregnant after the shadow of an otter has passed over them.

July

1

2

3

4

5

6

7

8

Fifteenth-century Irish story

the CHILDREN OF LIR

were changed to swans by a stepmother
jealous of their father's love.
they were sentenced to live
900 years on lake & sea
until returned to human form
by a saint at the moment of
their death.

Though I've yet a fish's tail
I'm not unbeautiful:
my hair is long and yellow
and there's a shine
from my scales
you won't see on
landlocked women.
Their eyes are like
the stones
But look into these
eyes of mine
and you will see
the sturgeon
and you will see
fine seals
gamboling
in my pupils.

9

10

11

12

13

14

15

16

from "An Mhaighdean Mhara" ["The Mermaid"] by Nuala Ní Dhomhnaill
twentieth century
trans. Michael Hartnett

July

17

18

19

20

21

22

23

24

Incident from the Irish epic, *Táin Bó Cuailgne* [*The Cattle Raid of Cooley*]
eighth century or earlier

Cuchulainn's Death!

Foreshadowed

when he reluctantly accepts dog meat from two hags, thereby violating a taboo forbidding him to eat the meat of the animal from whom he takes his name.

There were two golden tresses on her head, plaited in four, with a ball at the end of every lock. The color of her hair was like the flower of the iris in summer or like pure gold after it had been polished.

July

25

26

27

28

29

30

31

from "Tochmharc Étaíne" ["The Wooing of Étaín"], Anonymous
ninth century
trans. Myles Dillon

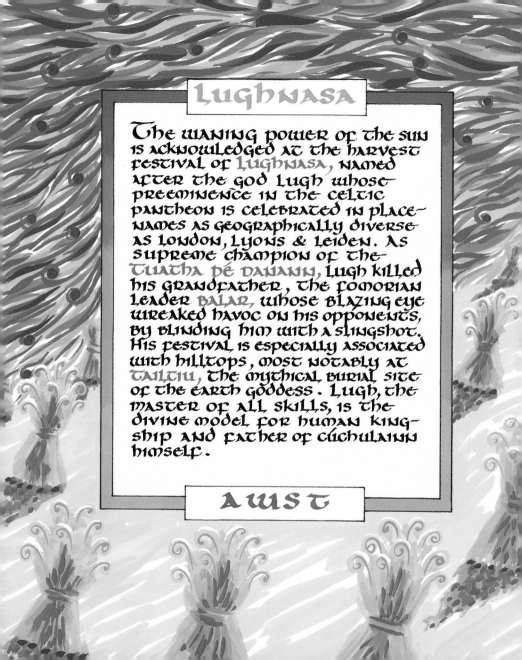

LUGHNASA

The waning power of the sun is acknowledged at the harvest festival of LUGHNASA, named after the god Lugh whose preeminence in the Celtic pantheon is celebrated in place-names as geographically diverse as London, Lyons & Leiden. As supreme champion of the TUATHA DÉ DANANN, Lugh killed his grandfather, the Fomorian leader BALAR, whose blazing eye wreaked havoc on his opponents, by blinding him with a slingshot. His festival is especially associated with hilltops, most notably at TAILTIU, the mythical burial site of the earth goddess. Lugh, the master of all skills, is the divine model for human king-ship and father of Cúchulainn himself.

AUST

August

1 _____

2 _____

3 _____

4 _____

5 _____

6 _____

7 _____

8 _____

from "Autumn," Anonymous
eighth century or earlier
trans. Frank O'Connor

Even the
spiky thorn-
bush growing
by the old deserted
fortress
staggers
with its weight
of berries,
hazelnuts
thud in the
forest from
the wearied
boughs.

THE·LID·WAS·RAISED·FROM·BALAR'S·EYE.

Then Lugh cast a sling-stone at him, which drove the eye through his head, and it was gazing on his own host. ◉ He fell on top of the Fomhóire army, so that thrice nine of them died under his side.

9

10

11

12

13

14

15

16

from *Cath Maige Tuired* [*The Battle of Moytirra*]
eleventh century

August

17

18

19

20

21

22

23

24

from *Cath Maige Tuired* [*The Battle of Moytirra*]
eleventh century

SMITH

WARRIOR

CHAMPION

When denied entry to the ROYAL COURT OF

TARA

where each skill he possessed was already represented among the heroes within,

Lugh

asked the doorkeeper which among them had all the skills together whereupon he was admitted to the feast.

BRAZIER

HARPER

HISTORIAN

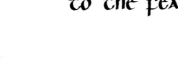
WRIGHT

CUPBEARER

PHYSICIAN

MAGICIAN

POET

MY

GRANDFATHER'S
SCYTHE

speal mo sheanathar

RUSTING IN
THE BARN—

ag meirgiú sa scíoból—

HARVEST
TWILIGHT

clapsholas fómhair

August

25

26

27

28

29

30

31

"Haiku" by Cathal Ó Searcaigh
twentieth century
trans. Gabriel Fitzmaurice

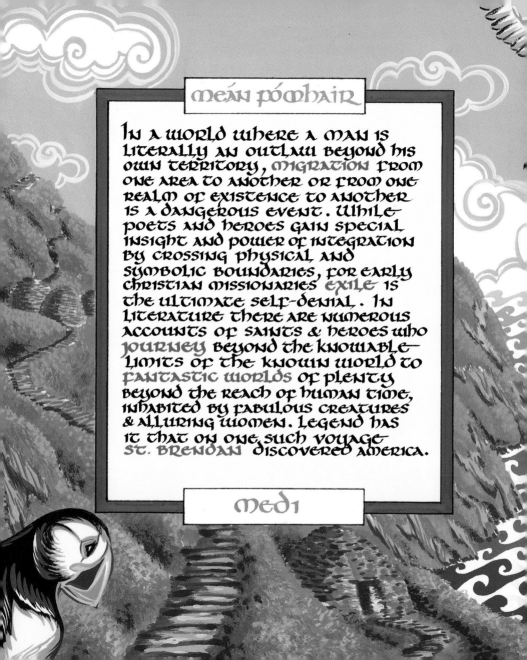

MEÁN FÓMHAIR

In a world where a man is literally an outlaw beyond his own territory, MIGRATION from one area to another or from one realm of existence to another is a dangerous event. While poets and heroes gain special insight and power of integration by crossing physical and symbolic boundaries, for early Christian missionaries EXILE is the ultimate self-denial. In literature there are numerous accounts of saints & heroes who JOURNEY beyond the knowable limits of the known world to FANTASTIC WORLDS of plenty beyond the reach of human time, inhabited by fabulous creatures & alluring women. Legend has it that on one such voyage ST. BRENDAN discovered America.

MEDI

September

1 _____

2 _____

3 _____

4 _____

5 _____

6 _____

7 _____

8 _____

based on the Irish-Gaelic manuscript, *The Life of Saint Brendan,* by
Michael O'Clery, dated 1629
trans. Charles Plummer

Seven years in all were they on the voyage—fair was the band—seeking the land of promise....

RAN'S SHIP IS REVELLING

IN A CLEAR SEA, BUT
TO ME, IN MY CHARIOT,
IT IS A FLOWERY PLAIN.
IN MY GENTLE LAND,...
SEA HORSES GLISTEN IN
THE SUN AND RIVERS
POUR FORTH HONEY.
FLOWERS ARE GROWING
WHERE BRAN SEES WAVES.

September

9

10

11

12

13

14

15

16

from "Immram Bhrain" ["The Voyage of Bran"]
eighth century
trans. Marie Heaney
Mannanán Mac Lir, god of the sea, speaks to Bran Feabhail
on his voyage to the otherworld.

September

17

18

19

20

21

22

23

24

from *Immram* [*The Voyage*], Part 3, "Hy-Breasil"
by Nuala Ní Dhomhnaill
twentieth century
trans. Paul Muldoon

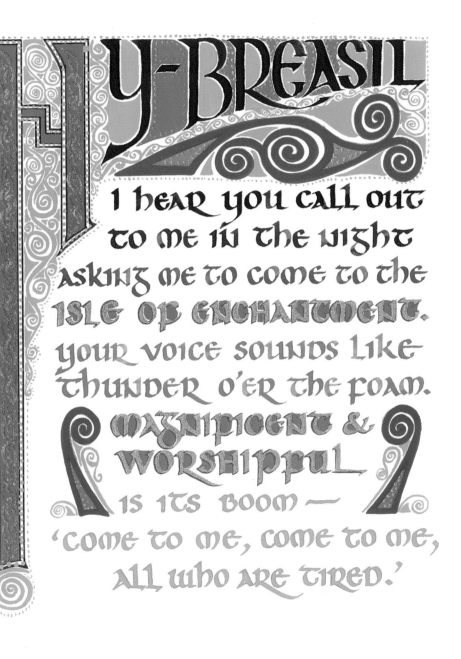

Hy-Breasil

I hear you call out
to me in the night
asking me to come to the
ISLE OF ENCHANTMENT.
your voice sounds like
thunder o'er the foam.
MAGNIFICENT &
WORSHIPFUL
is its BOOM —
'come to me, come to me,
all who are tired.'

I came, on my glorious adventure,

to a wondrous homestead... In that house
are the two kings, Fáilbe Finn & Labraid.
Each of them has a retinue of three fifties.
The one house holds all those people...
There is a border of blood-red beds, with
posts which are white & topped with gold...
Where the sun sinks...is a stud of grey
horses with many-coloured manes...To the
east, three trees of red glass stand...
There is a tree before the enclosure...a
silver tree upon which the sun shines...
In that fairy dwelling there is also a well
which holds thrice fifty many-coloured
cloaks... There is a vat there of merry mead
...It lasts forever unceasingly... And
there is a maiden in the house who has
excelled the women of Ireland...the hearts
of all break with longing & love for her...
Were all Ireland mine along with the
kingdom of bright Brega, I would give
it (no weak resolve) to dwell in the
homestead to which I came.

September

25

26

27

28

29

30

"Lóeg's Description to Cúchulainn of Labraid's Home in Mag Mell," Anonymous
eleventh century
trans. Gerard Murphy
Suffering a wasting sickness, Cúchulainn is invited to Mag Mell,
"The Plain of Delights," and sends his charioteer, Lóeg, ahead of him.

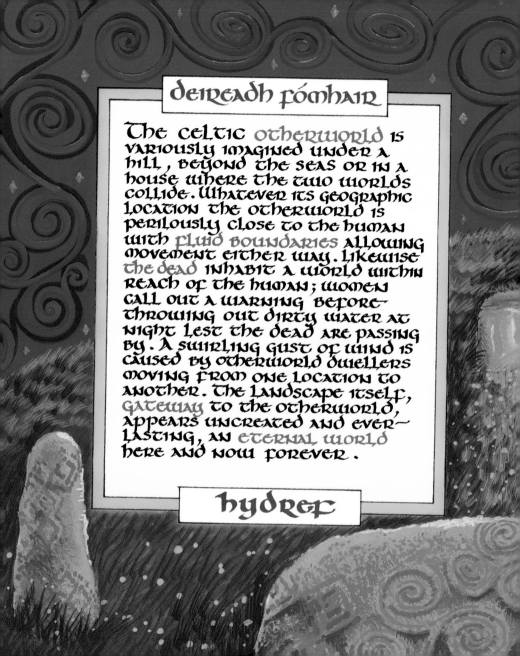

deireadh fómhair

The Celtic OTHERWORLD is variously imagined under a hill, beyond the seas or in a house where the two worlds collide. Whatever its geographic location the otherworld is perilously close to the human with FLUID BOUNDARIES allowing movement either way. Likewise the dead inhabit a world within reach of the human; women call out a warning before throwing out dirty water at night lest the dead are passing by. A swirling gust of wind is caused by otherworld dwellers moving from one location to another. The landscape itself, GATEWAY to the otherworld, appears uncreated and ever-lasting, an ETERNAL WORLD here and now forever.

hydref

October

1

2

3

4

5

6

7

8

"The King of Connaught," Anonymous
eighth century or earlier
trans. Frank O'Connor

"have you seen hugh, the Connacht king in the field?"

"All that we saw was his shadow under his shield."

When Cúldubh stole a half-cooked pig from the Fianna, Fionn pursued him to the sidh at Feimhean and speared him as he entered the otherworld. As Fionn tried to enter the mound, a woman on the other side closed the door on his thumb. From that time Fionn gained insight by sucking on the thumb that had entered the Otherworld.

October

9

10

11

12

13

14

15

16

Eighth-century story of Fionn Mac Cumhaill

October

17

18

19

20

21

22

23

24

from "An Bhatráil" ["The Battering"] by Nuala Ní Dhomhnaill
twentieth century
trans. Paul Muldoon

I only just made it home last night with my child from the fairy fort ...

Of the three wet nurses back in the fort, two had already suckled him:

had he taken so much as a sip from the third

That's the last I'd have seen of him ...

WILL STOP NOW—
my death is hurrying
near now the dragons
of the Leamhan, Loch Léin
& the Laoi are destroyed.

IN THE GRAVE
with this cherished
chief i'll join those
kings my people
served before the
death of Christ.

October

25

26

27

28

29

30

31

from "Cabhair ní Ghairfead" ["No Help I'll Call"] by Aogán Ó Rathaille
eighteenth century
trans. Thomas Kinsella

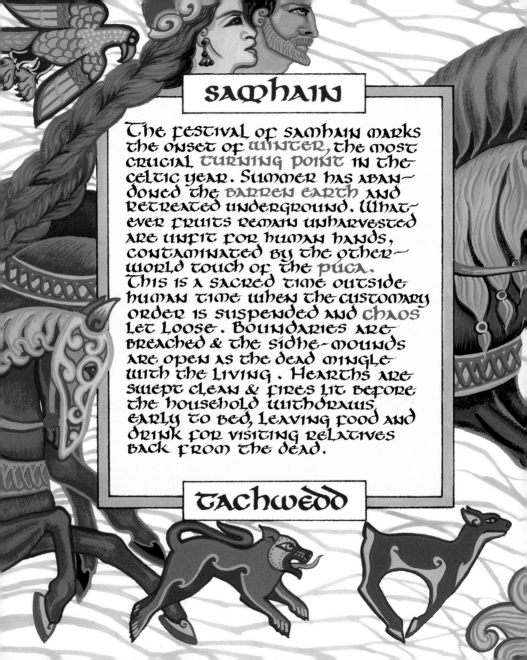

SAMHAIN

The festival of Samhain marks the onset of WINTER, the most crucial TURNING POINT in the Celtic year. Summer has abandoned the BARREN EARTH and retreated underground. Whatever fruits remain unharvested are unfit for human hands, contaminated by the otherworld touch of the PUCA. This is a sacred time outside human time when the customary order is suspended and CHAOS let loose. Boundaries are breached & the sidhe-mounds are open as the dead mingle with the living. Hearths are swept clean & fires lit before the household withdraws early to bed, leaving food and drink for visiting relatives back from the dead.

TACHWEDD

November

1

2

3

4

5

6

7

8

"Scél Lemm Dúib" ["News I Bring"]
ninth century

I HAVE NEWS FOR YOU:
THE STAG BELLS,
WINTER SNOWS,
SUMMER HAS GONE.

WIND HIGH AND COLD,
THE SUN LOW,
SHORT ITS COURSE,
THE SEA RUNNING HIGH.

DEEP RED THE BRACKEN,
ITS SHAPE IS LOST,
THE WILD GOOSE HAS RAISED
ITS ACCUSTOMED CRY.

COLD HAS SEIZED
THE BIRD'S WINGS;
SEASON OF ICE,
THIS IS MY NEWS.

EVERY BAY IN IRELAND BOOMS
WHEN THE FLOOD AGAINST IT COMES—
WINTER
THROWS
A SPEAR OF
FIRE!
ROUND SCOTLAND'S SHORES
AND BY CANTYRE
A MOUNTAINOUS SURGING
CHAOS GLOOMS.

November

9 _____

10 _____

11 _____

12 _____

13 _____

14 _____

15 _____

16 _____

from "Storm at Sea," ascribed to Rumann Mac Colmáin
eighth century
trans. Frank O'Connor

November

17
_____

18
_____

19
_____

20
_____

21
_____

22
_____

23
_____

24
_____

from "Winter," Anonymous
eighth century or earlier
trans. Frank O'Connor

CHILL chill!

all moylurg is cold &
still, where can deer
a-hungered go when
the snow lies like a hill?

The old eagle

of glen rye, even he
forgets to fly, with
ice crusted on his beak,
he is now too weak to cry.

The old house,
with skeletal grace,
is making music of
the wind:
without door or window
or the shelter of slates,
every wound is a
tin whistle
making wild
music

November

25

26

27

28

29

30

from "Fothrach Tí i Mín na Craoibhe" ["Ruin of House in Mín na Craoibhe"]
by Cathal Ó Searcaigh
twentieth century
trans. Thomas McCarthy

The need to reconcile conflicting opposites without denying the underlying tensions is a recurrent motif in celtic mythology where equilibrium of sorts can be achieved between the human and the natural, the masculine and feminine, between this and the otherworlds. The land itself integrates the rough places of strife & contention in Conn's half to the north with the waterfalls of Mogh's half in the south, home of poetry & music. Following the round of the agricultural year with its patterns of recurrence & renewal, the major festivals of the celtic calendar celebrate a cyclical notion of neverending time where every end is another beginning.

RHAGFYR

December

1
_____ ::

2
_____ ::

3
_____ ::

4
_____ ::

5
_____ ::

6
_____ ::

7
_____ ::

8
_____ ::

"Sneachta" ["Snow"] by Nuala Ní Dhomhnaill
twentieth century
trans. Michael Hartnett

NO BIRD SANG ◆ NO STAG SPOKE ◆ NO SEAL ROARED ◆ NO WAVE BROKE

In
the
winter
whiteness
of
the
hills
thatch eaves
are
heavy
with
frost—
from
their
teats,
silence
drips.

December

9

10

11

12

13

14

15

16

from "Séasúir" ["Seasons"] by Cathal Ó Searcaigh
twentieth century
trans. Gabriel Fitzmaurice

December

17

18

19

20

21

22

23

24

from "Amergin's Songs," Anonymous
tenth century
trans. Thomas Kinsella

I am Wind on Sea

I am Wave in Storm

I am Sea Sound & Seven-Horned Stag

I am Hawk on Cliff

A Drop of Dew in the Sun.

My hand
has a pain
from writing,
not steady
the sharp tol of my
CRAFT
its slender beak
spews bright ink—
a beetle-dark
shining
DRAUGHT.

December

25

26

27

28

29

30

31

from "Sgíth mo chrob ón sgríbinn" ["My hand has a pain from writing"]
ascribed to St. Columcille who died in 597
trans. Brian O'Nolan

Notes

Notes

ACKNOWLEDGMENTS

Thanks are extended to the copyright holders in the excerpts reproduced here. Details of sources follow.

Osborn Bergin (tr.): "Fuar liom an adhaighsi dh'Aodh" ["Too cold I deem this night for Hugh"] by Eochaidh Ó hEóghusa from *Irish Bardic Poetry*, Dublin Institute for Advanced Studies. Courtesy of the Governing Board of the School of Celtic Studies of the Dublin Institute for Advanced Studies.

James Carney (tr.): "An Droighneán Donn" ['The Blackthorn Bush"] from *Medieval Irish Lyrics*, Dolmen Press. Courtesy Colin Smythe Ltd.

Louis de Paor (tr.): "Mise Éire" ["I am Ireland"] by Pádraig Mac Piarais from *The Literary Writings of Patrick Pearse: Writings in Irish*, collected and edited by Séamus Ó Buachalla, Mercier Press , P. O. Box No. 5, Cork City, Ireland.

Myles Dillon (tr.): "Tochmharc Étaíne" [The Wooing of Étaín] from *Irish Sagas,* edited by Miles Dillon, published by Mercier Press, P. O. Box No. 5, Cork City, Ireland.

Samuel Ferguson (tr.): "Caiseal Mumhan" ["Cashel of Munster"] from *Poems of Samuel Ferguson,* Allen Figgis, Dublin.

Jeffrey Gantz (tr.): "The Destruction of Da Derga's Hostel" from *Early Irish Myths and Sagas* , Penguin Classics, 1981. Copyright ©Penguin Books Ltd, 1981. Reproduced by permission of Penguin Books Ltd.

Marie Heaney (tr.): "Immram Bhrain" ["The Voyage of Bran"] from *Over Nine Waves: A Book of Irish Legends,* Faber and Faber Ltd.

Brendan Kennelly (tr.): "Saint Brigid's Prayer" from *Love of Ireland: Poems from the Irish,* Mercier Press, P. O. Box No. 5, Cork City , Ireland.

Kinsella Thomas (tr.): "Amergin's Songs" from *New Oxford Book of Irish Verse,* Oxford University Press; "Binn Sin, a Luin Doire an Chairn!" [Beautiful Blackbird of Doire an Chairn!] and "Cabhair ní Ghairfead" ["No Help I'll Call"] by Aogán Ó Rathaille from *Poems of the Dispossessed*, Dolmen Press; *Táin Bó Cuailgne* [*The Cattle Raid of Cooley*] from *The Tain*, Oxford University Press. Courtesy Thomas Kinsella and Oxford University Press.

Proinsias Mac Cana, *Celtic Mythology*, Newnes Books, Hamlyn Publishing Group, Feltham, 1983. Extract courtesy Octopus Publishing Group Ltd.

Gerard Murphy (tr.): "Lóeg's Description to Cúchulainn of Labraid's Home in Mag Mell" from *Early Irish Lyrics*, Oxford University Press.

Nuala Ní Dhomhnaill: "An Bhatráil" ["The Battering"], trans. Paul Muldoon; *Immram* [*The Voyage*], Part 3, "Hy-Breasil," trans. Paul Muldoon. Both from *The Astrakhan Cloak*, the Gallery Press, Loughcrew, Oldcastle, Co. Meath, Ireland. "Blodewedd," trans. John Montague, from *Pharaoh's Daughter*, the Gallery Press, Loughcrew, Oldcastle, Co. Meath, Ireland. "An Mhaighdean Mhara" ["The Mermaid"], trans. Michael Hartnett; "I mBaile an tSléibhe" ["In Baile an tSléibhe"], trans. Nuala Ní Dhomhnaill; "Sneachta" ["Snow"], trans. Michael Hartnett. From *Selected Poems*, Nuala Ní Dhomhnaill, Raven Arts Press. Courtesy New Island Books, Dublin.

Flann O'Brien, *Myles before Myles*, Paladin, an imprint of Harper-Collins Publishers Limited. Extract used by permission of A.M. Heath & Co. Ltd on behalf of the Estate of the Late Brian O'Nolan.

Eamonn O Cannon(tr.): "Tir na nOg" by F. O'Connell from *Cuisle an Cheoil*, published by An Gum, Dublin,1976.

Frank O'Connor (tr.): "Aideen", "Autumn", "The Blackbird by Belfast Loch", "The King of Connaught", "May", "The Praise of Fionn", "Storm at Sea", "Táim Sínte ar do Thuama" ["I Am Stretched on Your Grave"] and "Winter". All from *Kings, Lords and Commons*, Gill & Macmillan, Dublin.Reprinted by permission of The Peters Fraser and Dunlop Group Limited on behalf of Frank O'Connor.

Dáithí Ó hÓgain, *Myth, Legend & Romance: An Encyclopaedia of the Irish Folk Tradition*, Prentice Hall Press, New York,1991.

Cathal Ó Searcaigh: "Cor Úr" ["A Fresh Dimension"], trans. Gabriel Fitzmaurice; "Fothrach Tí i Mín na Craoibhe" ["Ruin of House in Mín na Craoibhe"], trans. Thomas Mc Carthy; "Haiku," trans. Gabriel Fitzmaurice; "Séasúir" ["Seasons"], trans. Gabriel

Fitzmaurice and Cathal Ó Searcaigh. All from *An Bealach 'na Bhaile* [*Homecoming*] by Cathal Ó Searcaigh, Clo Iar-Chonnachta, Conamara, Co. Galway, Ireland.

Charles Plummer (tr.): *The Life of Saint Brendan* by Michael O'Clery from *Saint Brendan*, Floris Books, Edinburgh, 1992.

John Sharkey, *Celtic Mysteries: The Ancient Religion*, Thames & Hudson, London, 1975.

Lynne Muir was born in Melbourne and works as a freelance calligrapher and book illustrator. She has illustrated several award-winning picture books on Australian wildlife and regularly exhibits pieces of illuminated calligraphy. Her intricate paintings on parchment feature on birth certificates and official government citations. Lynne also sings in the traditional Celtic language and has recorded a rich selection of original and traditional Celtic folksongs, accompanying herself on the Appalachian Dulcimer and piano.

Louis de Paor is an Irish poet and academic. He has published prize-winning collections of poetry in both the Irish and English languages. His second collection was nominated in 1996 for the Irish Times Poetry Prize. He is currently working on a study of the work of Flann O'Brien.

First published 2007 by The O'Brien Press Ltd,
12 Terenure Road East, Rathgar, Dublin 6, Ireland.
Tel: +353 1 4923333; Fax: +353 1 4922777
E-mail: books@obrien.ie
Website: www.obrien.ie

ISBN: 978-1-84717-042-2

Originally published by Ten Speed Press

Illustrations copyright © 1999 Lynne Muir
Introduction and introductory notes copyright © 1999 Louis de Paor
Compilation and design copyright © 1999 Mallon Publishing Pty Limited
Endpapers: 'Tir na nOg' by F. O'Connell, trans. Eamonn O'Cannon

All rights reserved. No part of this publication may be reproduced or utilised
in any form or by any means, electronic or mechanical, including photocopying,
recording or in any information storage and retrieval system, without
permission in writing from the publisher.

British Library Cataloguing-in-Publication Data
Celtic book of days
1. Mythology, Celtic - Literary collections 2. Mythology,
Celtic 3. Diaries
I. De Paor, Louis, 1961- II. Muir, Lynne
299.1'6113

1 2 3 4 5
07 08 09 10 11

Printed by Tien Wah Press Ltd, Singapore

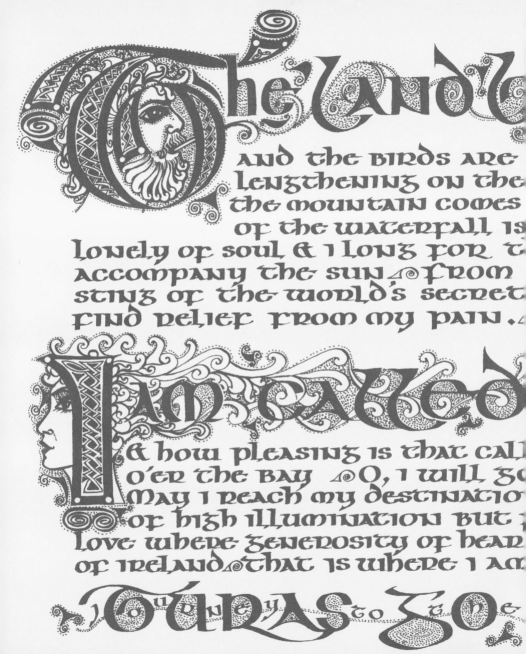

The land...

and the birds are
lengthening on the
the mountain comes
of the waterfall is
lonely of soul & I long for t
accompany the sun ☉ From
sting of the world's secret
find relief from my pain. ☉

I am called

& how pleasing is that call
o'er the bay ☉ O, I will go
may I reach my destinatio
of high illumination but
love where generosity of hear
of Ireland ☉ that is where I am

Journeys to Zoe